HARD WATER

HARD WATER

Jean Sprackland

CAPE POETRY

Published by Jonathan Cape 2003

2 4 6 8 10 9 7 5 3 1

First published in Great Britain in 2003 by
Jonathan Cape
Random House, 20 Vauxhall Bridge Road,
London SW1V 2SA

Random House Australia (Pty) Limited
20 Alfred Street, Milsons Point, Sydney,
New South Wales 2061, Australia

Random House New Zealand Limited
18 Poland Road, Glenfield,
Auckland 10, New Zealand

Random House South Africa (Pty) Limited
Endulini, 5A Jubilee Road, Parktown 2193, South Africa

The Random House Group Limited Reg. No. 954009
www.randomhouse.co.uk

A CIP catalogue record for this book
is available from the British Library

ISBN 0-224-06959-4

Papers used by Random House are natural,
recyclable products made from wood grown in sustainable forests;
the manufacturing processes conform to the environmental
regulations of the country of origin

Typeset by Palimpsest Book Production Limited, Polmont, Stirlingshire
Printed and bound in Great Britain by Biddles Ltd, Guildford & King's Lynn

For my mother and father

CONTENTS

ACKNOWLEDGEMENTS

Acknowledgements are due to the following publications: *Ambit, Boomerang, Critical Survey, London Review of Books, New Republic, Poetry London, Poetry Review, Smiths Knoll, Smoke, The Times Literary Supplement.*

The 'No Man's Land' sequence first appeared alongside photographs by David Walker at the Lowry Centre, Salford, in 2001.

Thanks to all those friends who have advised and encouraged me, including (too late) RB for the pencils.

I am grateful to the Hawthornden Trust for awarding me a fellowship in 2002.

HARD WATER

I tried the soft stuff on holiday in Wales,
a mania of teadrinking and hairwashing,
excitable soap which never rinsed away,

but I loved coming home to this.
Flat. Straight. Like the vowels,
like the straight talk: *hey up me duck.*
I'd run the tap with its swimming-pool smell,
get it cold and anaesthetic. Stand the glass
and let the little fizz of anxiety settle.
Honest water, bright and not quite clean.
The frankness of limestone, of gypsum,
the sour steam of cooling towers,
the alchemical taste of brewing.

On pitiless nights, I had to go for the bus
before last orders. I'd turn up my face,
let rain scald my eyelids and lips.
It couldn't lie. Fell thick
with a payload of acid. No salt –
this rain had forgotten the sea.
I opened my mouth, speaking nothing
in spite of my book-learning.
I let a different cleverness wash my tongue.
It tasted of work, the true taste
of early mornings, the blunt taste
of *don't get mardy*, of *too bloody deep for me*,
fierce lovely water that marked me for life
as belonging, regardless.

FIBRE OPTICS

The cables ran creaking off a ship
bound for our city. They slipped plumb-straight
through slots in the waves, sank weighted
through cooler and colder seams,
down into the dark where they met
their own kind: fishes with light inside them.
In that radiant company they made
a superhighway of the ocean floor.
Jellyfish, squid, sea-sponge go on
with their languageless lives, while light
pulses and flickers through plastic, a racket
of coded voices from a million places
to a million others, and back, and back again.

And when I want to make that journey myself
here's how I'll do it:
I'll slip under the sea's edge,
reach out and grasp the fibres.
I'll track the seabed, guided and saved by words,
by the unimportant and important things
people say to others like them
over unexplored and lethal distances.

SEACOAL

What redundant seam wasted this spoil?
His boots crunch lumps of it
ravelled with seaweed, sea-potatoes and starfish,
condoms and tampons, messages in bottles.
It's the ancient relative of all these,
he thinks, taking a piece and rubbing it
on his sleeve. It yields first a dark glint,
then a glassy shine. Washed and wholesome,
a chip of our drowned green past,
smoothed and blue-faceted by the sea.

A bucketful makes a damp fire,
sweating and spitting salt.
He throws on a log to kindle pictures
he notices are all of the sea.
He wakes shivering
by a grate of ash and clinker.
Prehistory is still there, under the ocean.

He steals a boat and diving gear.
The aqualung is his time machine.
And there it is: an undisturbed continent of trees.
The forest floor swells with life.
The canopy bubbles with birds and monkeys
adapted to life underwater.
There is sunlight in the crucible of leaves.

THE ROOM OF SAINTS AND VIRGINS

We're survivors, says Saint Joseph,
rattling the stump of his wooden arm
and the folds of his wooden cloak.

Saint Bieuzy turns his stone eyes on the dinosaur tooth,
the knapped flints, the frayed Roman coins,
the vestments of an eighteenth-century bishop.
Call this survival? We were better off
trodden by cattle, buried and bulldozed,
bitten by axe and shovel, mutilated by the plough.
We're scraps under the table now. Where's the faith?

Faith, sighs a decapitated plaster virgin,
spreading her hands illegibly.
I'd settle for a little shrine by a spring
and red stain for my lips.

Downstairs, the curator flicks off the lights
and buttons his coat against the rain,
thinking of whisky and television,
his plump landlady in a white slip.

READING LEAVES

A change of wind brings a few foreign leaves,
skimming the hedge and the dustbins,
landing on my lawn like splashes of blood.
I pick one up and try to read it, but the message
is in a language of reds I can't decipher.
Its texture is of folded money, suggesting
a climate of plenty, wild parrots, a generous sky.

I set off to find the source: south-west,
somewhere beyond the school and the shoe factory.
I follow the scent of warmth and wealth,
leaving the town centre, the municipal buildings.
Then I'm lost in a tract of tower-blocks
and boarded-up shops, a children's playground
with broken glass, the stump of a roundabout.
I carry my red leaf as a guarantee.
A young mother shrugs *Try the bloke in the hut –
he's not from round here either.*

He leans forward on the concrete bench,
takes the leaf in his palm, squints a long moment.
He speaks, and the wind freshens in reply.
Litter tumbles about the playground,
washing strung across balconies creaks and flaps.
And here they come: a flock of red leaves
circling, stepping down the grey air,
settling like rumours on his coat,
his boots, the bench, the broken ground.

CARAVAN

This is not about camels
bearing spices along a dusty contour
of the imagination, and sherbet,
and red and yellow silk

but a squarish sort of tin can
squat on the edge of a farmer's field:
nettles, stars, one cold tap.

Here you practise self-sufficiency
under a sheet-metal shelter;
assert a kind of integrity
via brown leatherette benches
which fold down into a bed;
calor gas; the neat double ring
where you cook a basic supper for two
and eat it all yourself.
You unfasten the plastic clip
and sit at the open window all day,
watching the sky lighten and darken,
the clouds part and regroup.

Let others go for something more upmarket:
thirty-six foot, six berth, cream with burgundy trim
and a name that means business –
The Challenger, The Marauder –
precision-parked on an exact pale
quota of grass like a slice of white bread,
at an intersection of rows and columns,
gravel paths and strimmed hedges,
with an electric hook-up, and neighbours.

There wouldn't be much to say:
Lovely morning. Keep it nice don't they.
And sometimes: *Quite a storm last night.*

Alone, you can let on
how much you like it:
the roll and sway of the van
on the wind's swell. The rain like marbles,
reassuring after all that silence.

LEARNING TO LOVE MONEY

It may not be to everyone's taste,
but this girl found money delicious.
During the sermon she'd rub the collection coin,
sniff her fingers, lick them,

she'd slip the coin in her mouth,
sucking very quietly and stopping
to give her mother a holy sort of smile.
All the filthy hands, the pockets,

think of the germs. But foreignness
was what this girl liked: the flavour
of other people's lives, lived somewhere else
in unimaginable ways

(she loved the word *change*
and would say it in shops whenever she could).

She brailled it with her tongue,
pressed it to the roof of her mouth,
felt the brain's circuitry
arch and prickle. News from beyond.

SHOCKS

Remember those first thrills, the charge
that went cracking through you?
Sunday afternoons we went out on our bikes,
me and next-door Julie.
She had black ringlets and a wicked smile.

We crossed the dual carriageway
like small determined animals swimming a swollen river.
Then out into the lanes. A dappled horse
shambled hopefully towards the gate.
We dropped our bikes on the verge,
took out apple cores and polo mints.
We pretended this was why we'd come.
We perched on the gate,
picking scabs of rust and telling secrets:
the time Derek Wesley saw a dead man
in the old air-raid shelter. The little packets
Julie found in her dad's wardrobe.

She always made the first move,
casual and bold by the electric fence.
She bet me anything it wasn't on.
Touch it. I dare you. I said it first.
The blood jittered in my fingertips,
my throat. I thought I could hear the current
singing in the cable. I reached out.

SEWING FINGERTIPS

Queuing at Miss Pope's desk
to have our cross-stitch checked,
we made daring needlework of our fingers
in moss green and golden brown.
More thrilling than those woven squares
where you followed the holes,
no piercing involved.

We were desperadoes, raising the stakes
by sewing ourselves to our jumpers,
to the pages of our jotters,
to each other.

Like firewalkers, or sleepers on beds of nails,
we vied and swaggered:
see my magic,
look how brave I am,
I never make a fuss.

Except the new girl,
weeping through clenched teeth,
hand embroidered with blood.
Learning what it means
to try too hard.

TELL YOUR MOTHER I SAVED YOUR LIFE

At the top of the stairs in the Science Block
you're shoved then grabbed back by your blazer.
The world tilts, your veins fizz.
Some boy and his goofy mates cackle behind you.
It's just a laugh, don't you get it?

This foreshadows new mysteries with boys
at parties or bus stops. You are forever guessing,
wrong-footed, checking the shadows
for his sniggering gang. He says something
which could mean this or that. He keeps not kissing you
then just as your bus arrives he changes his mind,
and you falter again at the top of that stairwell,
possessed, vertiginous. You sit at the back,
your head throbbing against the misted glass.

AN OLD FRIEND COMES TO STAY

She rings from a station
somewhere south of Heaven, north of here.
Guess what? I'm down for the weekend.
A sleeping bag on the sofa will do.
I'd forgotten the precise smoky register
of her voice, how close it is to jazz.

Good thing I kept her Indian cotton skirt,
the one I took when she died.
She arrives without luggage, wearing
temporary garments unsuitable for October.
She bundles the skirt to her face,
breathing its lost scent. I lend her
a red sweater – she was always glamorous in red –
but the wool makes her skin itch.
Bodies are so treacherous, she says,
allergies, wrinkles, wind . . .
I want to talk about the day we buried her
but it seems impossibly rude

so I ask has she got plans,
people to look up, business to finish?
She says by Christ she could murder a brandy and coke.
The band is loud and loose, the sax man
half her age, leather jeans and a ponytail.
I come back from the bar, and he's rolling her a cigarette.
She's telling him she's spent five years as pure spirit,
she's missed the pleasures of the flesh.

Well what did I think she'd want,
a day out at the Albert Dock?
She's travelled so far to get here
and forty-eight hours can be very short.
I'll get off home and leave the door on the latch.

NOTE FROM THE OUTSIDE

Here are busy streets of fish,
dead tower-blocks squatted by gulls.

When they dropped me off at the wood's edge
I was stammered by green,
I was torn to rags by the silence.
I walked like a bent pin,
stubbing my toes on the emptiness.

Remember that library book about the ocean?
You should see the night sky:
its buoys and lighthouses,
its flares and shipping lanes.

LIFESAVING

A woman walking this gorge with her husband
left the path to get a better photo –
at least that's what she said to him.
She crossed a shuddering bridge
over a waterfall where the mist made rainbows,
climbed down between trees and dripping dark
to a beach of flat rock
where the river shot past, sly and hungry.
The sun was warm here
and no one to ask what she was thinking.

A bubbling cry startled her,
the lost cry of someone at the limit, suspended
between one breath and the next.
A boy came racing towards her on the current,
arms beating the black water.
She knelt at the edge,
seized the swollen shoulders of his coat
and dragged him out onto the rock
where he lay waterlogged and mewling.
The woman stroked the water from his face.
The sun would work its magic on him now.
Her husband was calling her name
from beyond the bridge. She glanced back once
and walked briskly away upstream.

It's a prophecy as stern
as *The End of the World is Nigh*.
Office workers with mobiles and takeaway sandwiches
pause to feel the small cold thrill of their own mortality

before noticing that the tense is wrong,
everything has gone. A truck in the night,
the automatic door on override,
casual workers wheeling out trolleys of stock,
dismembered rails and shelves, computerised till
heaped on the pavement and slung aboard.
The tailgate banged shut and it was over.

It has happened here and it will happen everywhere:
a room stripped to dust and the drift of utility bills.
Huge windows still making desperate offers.

ST NICHOLAS AND THE SALTED BOYS

When I was sent to offer meat to the bishop,
he rose sharply, spilling the lamp.
Take me to this meat.
I stumbled as I led him down the cellar steps
to the great wooden brine-tub. Upstairs
I heard my master running from the house.

Open it. It was forbidden,
but the bishop's eyes were darker than the shadows.
I shoved the lid creaking like a church door,
heaved it crashing to the flagstones.

When I saw, I reeled away,
my chest burning with screams.
He touched my forehead, and I was cooled at once.
He made the Sign of the Cross, leaned in,
pulled streaming from the tub
first one naked boy, then a second and a third.

Those skinny sons of our famished village
stood like dreamers, bleached
and wizened by salt, each throat
slashed with a blue scar.
The bishop raised his hand in blessing.
Brine bled from his sleeve and pooled on the floor.

Fashions change. Once we lost our audience
no subsidy could bring it back.
Bums on seats is what counts in the end.
So I was out on my ear, looking to re-train.
Utilise your experience, Mr Slackitt,
says the girl at the Jobclub. *Transferable skills.*
I knew I had a sense of drama,
kept a cool head where another man might panic.
I'm quite a virtuoso when it comes to whistling.
I've seen the naked fear of people
who know the game is up, so I did a stint
with the Samaritans.

        But I missed the ropes.
Down at the harbour I found a few weeks' work
on the ferry, where I could coil the hawser,
feel the heat on my palm as I paid it out.
Some days I stayed on in the dusk
blunting my fingers on favourite
knots and hitches.

        Then I did this course
in Outdoor Pursuits. The kids are cocky
till you get one roped at the top of a cliff
and he stares with no colour in him,
just the giddy faith that you'll hold him. Yes
I miss the blindfold, the bang of the trapdoor,
the hiss and thud. But this time
it's my judgement that counts.
I balance my weight against his,
feed the rope through the karabiner, watch him
blunder the long drop and stagger on solid ground.

THE MAN WHO COMES TO EMPTY
THE BOTTLE BANK

brings bread to throw for the seagulls.
Rats on wings the boss calls them
but they remind him of holidays as a kid:
a week in Scarborough, salt on your lips.
The birds are a promise against
the endless catastrophe of this place –
the breaking, the hopeless sound of it,
the dead cats, the curdled air –

and later, as the chains tense
and the skip swings on the arm of the crane,
sunlight crackles across the surface
and he almost dives in. He could plunge
deep into that shattered sea, come up clean.

BEFORE THERE WERE
WEATHER FORECASTS

Before there were weather forecasts
three women working a cabbage field
were carried away by a great flood.
A man building a stone wall
was lost in a blizzard which rushed out of nowhere.
Whole crops were thumbed flat
by an angry wind, a retribution.
There had been a text in the stars
which no one had translated in time.

And in those days there was sickness too;
madness; sudden death from a fever
with no name. People found the reasons:
failure, heresy, sin. Recalled and repented.
Cause and effect were knots on a line
looping back through a lifetime, back
through generations, to the Fall.

Tonight the gritters are out, and a neighbour
is tucking nylon fleece around seedlings.
You should not drive unless your journey is essential.
Structural damage is likely, especially
here in your town, to your house.
But that bit of insider dealing, don't dwell on it.
The flesh you touched in a foreign city, forget it,
you'll never be traced. And there are no stars tonight.

THE LIGHT COLLECTOR

He knows broad daylight inside out,
can't get excited any more by the tawdry brilliance of it,
flattening everything, dumbing it down.
From an open window on the seventh floor
he watches the street scudding below, and thinks
I must make something of my life, as if it were
a bag of rags for recycling.
                    Gauzy scraps of dawn
have begun to bore him. He leans out
into the caramel light of late summer evening
smattering wet roofs and TV aerials: too rich, too obvious.

At night he daydreams tricks so bright
he feels they lend him context.
He knows he has a steady way with starlight,
can pick it up like sand on a fingertip.
He goes out under the moon, in the fabulous air
tasting of electricity. He lingers by houses with drawn curtains,
presses himself thin as a shadow and watches light
bleeding from the open doorway of a pub.
But it leaves him hungry. What he seeks
for his own broken purpose is smaller
more secretive sources: the bits you find
in the sweepings of a long day alone.
The cryptic blue cast by a computer. The smash-and-grab
of camera flash. The blade of light under the door
with voices glinting behind it.

He wants to stop all the draughts in this place
with light, he wants it to shed meaning.
In the dark kitchen he opens the fridge
and the light is so sweet and precise it leaves him aching.

SHADOW PHOTOGRAPH

On the run from our own faces,
but wanting to capture
the oddness of our conjunction,
we photographed our shadow:
a dark double figure on sand,
the negative we were together.

Earlier that day
he parked on the beach and parted my thighs,
the first to try and define me with his tongue.
He was not the one, it was all wrong.
I struggled against the seatbelt
and my damp, bunched skirt,
making to pull away, kick the door open,
scramble out into the sunlight

but suddenly loosened into stillness
by that silvery flickering,
the new low sound of my voice,
the sweetness leaking from me where he drank.

We intercepted light, we were
a region unreached by it.
This is the ghost of us,
a counterfeit holiday snap:
my head on his shoulder, some blown hair
like a dark flame.

LOSING THE DARK

November, when day should close early
like a dull book. But that afternoon
a small cloud in the shape of a question-mark
passed over the sun and dissolved.
Six o'clock; eight; ten. Daylight
still flooded the startled street.

Such a gift. Like one of those summer evenings
when you sit out, glass in hand,
under the darting flightpaths of swifts.
It opened faces, shops, back doors.
Sleep and secrets were like dusty fetishes;
we took midnight walks, made love in sunlit rooms.
Even on the seventh night, dreamless
and nervy, we couldn't foresee it:

this shoving and kicking for basements
and underground stations, away from the glare
that opens you like a knife. How all the birds
might sing themselves to death.

THE MISSION

We break into the cryonics centre
on a mission to liberate the dead.
We're dissidents, still believing in beginnings
and ends. The place is razor-wired
but we've got Jed, fresh from freeing lab monkeys.
The stuff he tells us – electrodes, viruses –
makes my teeth rattle. He cuts us in
and we go flat on our bellies
over the grass, the early crocuses.

In the warehouse the giant flasks hum.
Jed forces the door and throws the switches
and there's a massive sigh of electrical
disappointment, or relief. A thaw will soon set in.
Frozen cells will flood, muscles collapse,
all the dammed-up death will flow again.
They're stored upside-down,
so the brain stays frozen in powercuts.
We lay some flasks on the floor and lever them open.
One is a child, bruised and wide-eyed.

They call it *suspension*, like holding a video on pause.
Wait for science to mend the broken,
cure the rotten, replace, rewire, jumpstart.
Help them to their feet and see them off the premises.
The iron gates clang shut behind them.

Then think of it: everyone you know is gone,
your great-great-grandchildren are gone,
your home is demolished, your neighbourhood erased,
every detail unimaginably different.
You stumble towards the edge of town
in your ramshackle body, aching for a familiar
voice or touch, but you're a ghost
for all this new world cares. Perhaps
you've sometimes felt a little like this? Then you'll know it:
in spite of all the bargaining,
the dead just want to be dead.

A BABY IN THE FILING CABINET

bursts the room with its crying,
rips you apart at the breastbone
and pins you out on the nylon carpet.
It's all shuddering steel echo,
all blowtorch rage.
It drags in static and blows out despair.

The computer screen spits and flickers in response,
the papers on your desk billow and scoot to the floor.
The phone rings, and stops. Rings, and stops.
The words in your head
screw themselves out through your ears, and escape.
Your city clothes melt with your sweat.

When it stops you open the drawers
one by one, but there's nothing there.
Big shattering nothing.
You kneel with your head on the cool metal.
You'd climb in there yourself
if only they made the things to fit.

THE APPRENTICE

I married a big man with clumsy hands,
whose touch left me fingerprinted with bruises.
I had to keep him from my bed
till he learned some delicacy.
I wanted him dextrous

so I trained him on nimble tasks. First time
hanging out washing, he snapped a dozen pegs,
let underwear fall in the wet grass.

Then I had him sowing lettuces,
pricking out the seedlings, growing them on.
He was close to tears with the smallness of the work.

I schooled him in needle and thread,
a hard apprenticeship in gentleness.
He fumbled the button, knocked the licked end of thread
against the stubborn eye of the needle,
stabbed his fingertip. Blood on his white shirt.

One night, after dinner, the final test:
unfastening my silver necklace.
When I felt those skilful fingers
lift my hair and charm the tiny clasp apart,
I stood astonished, sheened in desire. I turned
and took his hands, set them free.

LOVE-SONG TO A PARKING METER

Good, the street's quiet,
I can run my hands all over you.
Crisp edges, cold smooth planes,
slot shining and ready. Once someone had wedged
a slice of cucumber in there. The shame.

You give me exactly what I pay for:
two pounds sixty for one hour.
No debts run up, no favours,
no strings attached. We deal together
cleanly and without coercion.

I never suffer flights of fancy
about a little man crouching inside you,
taking the money, keeping count. What I see, I like:
Your privet–green satin finish.
Your plain glass dial.
Your dignity, your fair play.

Someone has written on your side:
Dez is Sex on Legs.
I understand the need to tell you secrets.
Sometimes I wrap my arms around you,
bend close till my lips touch the cool of you.
I tell you how it is for me
here in this feverish city
under an unstable sky.
Your steady ticking is the only response I need.
Oh you are solidly mounted.
I rock against you, but you stand firm.

YEAST

You can get drunk on the air
in this town. There's a wild smell
the locals love: malt, hops

and yeast, which is tricky stuff,
doesn't like to be controlled.
Microscopic spores escape from the breweries,
filling the air with excitement.
Carried all over town, they find out sugar
and corrupt it. You open a cupboard
and find marmalade transfigured
into froth, spreading over shelves,
dripping spoilt and heady.

Saccharomyces cerevisiae.
It spreads like scandal,
creating bubbles of discontent
wherever there's a bit of sweetness.
It makes things unstable.
Even places you'd think were safe
– a home, a bed   disordered.
The song of a blackbird
exaggerates a restless night
and you wake, feverish,
ready to make something happen. Anything.

THE SECRET

I know a woman who has sex with men
then works magic which makes them forget.
It's not me, I assure you.
It's a friend who tells me everything.

The thrill of seduction, time and again,
whenever she wants it. The heartstopping moment
when he reaches to unbutton her shirt,
his voice thick with desire – *I've wanted this for months* –
or silent in the full beam of her eyes.
It's not the freeze-frame and replay of memory
but a swarm of possibilities, nothing precluded.

And she picks up men
in late-night bars, museums, business meetings,
in Woolworths, at the school gate. No need to be frugal
now there's no such thing as consequence.
She gets drunk with them, tells them dark truths
or white lies, asks precise and clever questions
about their work, their wives,
and this is all they remember next day:
a woman who showed an interest.

It's safe to be animal with them.
She slicks herself on their mouths.
She licks the sweat from their skin,
spreads out like a starfish in the current.
She sucks the secret heat from them.

Afterwards, the magic. Don't ask me what it is.
This woman tells me everything, but I gave a promise.

If the sex was disappointing, it's dropped,
and no awkwardness. This way
she stays clean and free and hurts no one.
He sees her again, at the office or in the street,
and smiles. He wonders what she looks like naked.

I can see by your face you think she's me.
No. She's a good friend.
Now let's talk about you.

THE LAST CIGARETTE

I enjoy the slow ritual of selecting one,
tapping it on the wall,
putting it to my lips
and tasting the raw malty scent.
At home, my wife will be taking off her nightdress,
assessing her red eyes in the mirror.

Under the gaze of the firing squad,
the guard strikes a match and shelters the flame.
I make him wait
while I scuff at a spent cartridge on the ground.
The plum tree in our garden will be flowering now
but there was a frost again this morning.

In my own time I turn and accept the light.
Then the first long draw, the blue
finger of smoke opening my throat
and spreading its glamour in my chest.
In a distant suburb: a siren. A man
will be thrashing free of a dark dream of his guilt.

Drag after deep drag. Then
I smudge out the stub on the pockmarked wall,
toss it down and finish it at last
with the toe of my boot. I look up with a smile.
In a sunlit kitchen, our baby will be finding the trick
with tongue and teeth and making his first word.

TEACHING FROGS TO FLY

In my friend Suzy's garden
the lawn is soft and even as Axminster,
the crazy paving is scrubbed to a shine
and the pond is for goldfish only.
One hot day, Suzy's dad dips a net
and scoops out a frog.
It scrambles, kicking a wisp of green lace.
He plucks it with finger and thumb
by one ridiculous leg, and grins. *Ready for take-off!*
A thrill of cruelty and shame
ripples the hairs on my arms.
Then the frog is a small toy, arcing
against the blue, over the fence
into the field by the woods.
I can't see it fall, but he says it's a personal best.

When he's gone indoors,
Suzy stretches on the sun-bed,
her skin glistening like Everlasting Toffee Strip.
I hear a faint croak from the end of the garden.
Oh they always come back, she says.
She tells me to take off all my clothes
and pretend to be her boyfriend, Sacha Distel.
I think of the frog scenting that silky water,
those prosperous fish. It couldn't resist.
No need to tramp off in my wellies and rescue it
when everyone else has gone in for tea.
Suzy's dad is a hero, a genius.
He's teaching frogs to fly.

SLEEP

In the middle of ice cream
your son just stops, slumps forward,
a thread of raspberry sauce
at the corner of his mouth

and you nudge him
and rattle his spoon because
the magic show will be starting
and he wants to see the white rabbit, remember?

But he's heavy with sleep,
his face closed and forgetting.
Your own sleep now is as thin and brittle
as a layer of burnt sugar

and your fantasies are all of letting go,
of your own warm hand between your thighs,
of pillows and the weight of blankets,
clean sheets

where you would stretch out to occupy
your defensible space, exercise
your selfish right whenever you want to,
going all the way

down, and down, into the warm
salty myth of yourself,
falling back into your own blood,
your heart keeping its soft permissive watch

and you folded inside
your unbroken skin, spinning such slow webs:
diving through thorny tunnels leading
to a lake with a perfect surface

or rising like smoke,
swimming endless spirals
in a shimmering emptiness so blue
you could come in your sleep.

MR SMILEY

There's a man the local kids call Mr Smiley
but if they smile at him he flinches,
he walks in the road to avoid them.
To him people are the clothes they stand in,
the dangerous shapes and noises they make.
(Trees are quieter and more predictable.)

This man catches a train twice a day. It's easy,
like water running when you turn on a tap,
like the six o'clock news.
But when a train runs late he trembles
and sometimes the train sits ticking in a dark tunnel
and his head is loud with fear.
The circling of the earth alarms him:
he owns a calendar
but seasons come and go raggedly.

He knows more than his share of things:
calculus, the names of newly discovered stars,
the capital cities. He has an interest
in garden gates with their wrought iron scrolls,
their many styles of latch.
His drawings are clean and precise,
not grubby with involvement or desire.

He carries one bag of clothes to the launderette
on Saturday at ten, fetches them home at three.
Dishes washed, shoes polished and paired.
Still his mother cries for him. She's like the rest of us:
rotten with longing and striving
and scuffing each other raw.
And all she wants is for him to be like that.

SYNCHRONISED DROWNING

When I give the signal
the glamour begins.
Let the cold curtain
fold over you.
Tread the space heavily
and beat a froth with your arms.
You can be confident
that my movements are mirroring yours.
Open your mouth on water
slick with small jelly life;
feel your tongue swimming
with microscopic fear.
The important thing is precision
and a bright smile.
Open your lungs
and breathe green air
stranded with weed.
Relax. After all that practice
our timing is bound to be good.
Let the mud floor tug you.
Take a last look at sunlight
streaking the oily surface above.
Roll your eyes and sing with me
a steady diminuendo of bubbles.

THE HAIRDRESSER'S
ACROSS THE STREET

When they're alone and think no one's watching
some of the customers pick up the bottles,
unscrew them and sniff.
They lean towards the mirror and look at their teeth.
When the stylist comes back they're always
idling through *Homes & Gardens* or *Hello*.

Today a woman with a white perm
has been having it washed. I've been watching
the way her hair is so much longer wet.
His hands were bunching it and raking it loose
under the tap. Then he left the room.

He was gone and gone. The woman was alone,
with her head back in the cut-away basin.
Do you know how it feels
to be left like that, the water running off your hair?
You don't like to sit up and call for service.
A few bubbles fizz close to your ear.
You start to shiver. The muscles are tight
in the back of your neck,
your throat arched and naked.
Swallowing your own saliva
is like swallowing rocks.

I watch the woman till I think she must be asleep
in that back-to-front black nylon cape. She's so still
I wonder whether she's dead.
If the stylist doesn't get off the phone soon
he'll forget her, and she'll still be there
when he grabs his jacket, sets the alarm
and locks the place shut behind him.

The tick of the cooling dryers into the dusk.
Her hair dripping slow, slower.

BARBIE ON THE ROOF

Barbie is on the roof, naked,
wasting her smile on the heartless sky.
Rain drums on her hollow body, her hair
a splintering of nylon on the dark tiles.

That's where the boy threw her
beyond his sister's reach
even as she leant out of the bedroom window,
stretching till her fingers ached.

They were too much together, Barbie and his sister,
too long in happy-ever-after.
Aerobics. Motorhome. Kitchen. Wedding dress.
It was hot indoors and out, and he was alone.

Now it's winter. The girl grooms plastic ponies
and keeps the window shut. Barbie sprawls on the roof,
her dangerous legs at the wrong angles,
one cracked hand raised in hopeful surrender.

AND THEY ALL LIVED
HAPPILY EVER AFTER

Someone has smeared a whitewash pattern
like clouds
on the window of the empty flat

though there's nothing to see inside, except
the sad glitz of shooting up,
the fast illicit fuck. A hallway

littered with condoms and silver foil.
But it's the best-looking window on the block:
no metal shutter, no jagged glass, yet,

just this cloudscape, a smudged reminder
of the picturebook clouds
you watch from an aeroplane window

as you surf the sunlit nowhere and feel
unlimited again. Like something from a story
deep in the marrow of you:

a room where straw is spun into gold,
a gingerbread house,
a handful of worthless beans.

There's something hopeful about this window,
something which says we can go back after all,
there's enough gold to buy back the cow,

and the thick page turning under the circle of light,
and the warm cream of that voice, and an arm
reaching across to pull the covers up.

MAGIC

She gripped a rough ball
of silver paper in her fist

for when she had to pass
bigger kids on new bikes.

Squeezing it in her fingers
would keep her safe.

But that afternoon in the lane,
when a car crept alongside

and stopped, she scrabbled nothing
but empty fluff in her pocket.

Without her amulet how could she
counter the strange jinx

in his lap: all the bad magic
she'd ever dared to imagine.

HOLY

It is written in the book of saints that Our Lady
appeared to me in a waterfall near Combret
and that through me she fed the hungry of that town.
No one however speaks of the child I bore
by the priest at Millau where I continued my work.
I wish you to know how first I guided his hands.
I was a torrent he rode like a raft, I surged
beneath him and leapt at last, speechless,
like a writhing fish. This too should be recorded

but my passions are of course eclipsed
by the table I kept for the poor: meat and bread,
sustenance for the sick and the outcast.
God was bountiful. As my belly swelled
I held fast to the work: carrying food to the cellars
where beggars scuttled like rats,
to the caves near the river where madmen lived.
My pale unworldly looks they took for innocence

but I was fruitful. By the river
I cried to Our Lady to deliver me;
I split like a damson and yielded a son,
lay all night with him pressed to my shivering.
In the morning, I wrapped him in rags and left him
at the cave's mouth, where I knew he'd be found
and brought to me as an orphan.

Write down in your book that this woman of Christ
heard too the Word of the flesh.
Tell how the milk sprang from my breasts,
how the poor smiled at my singing
as I set warm loaves before them.

TRANSLATING BIRDSONG

The whole mix of different sounds is a symphony of the unknown.
        Geoff Sample, *Garden Bird Songs and Calls*

I'm drawn to the happiness of birds.
They never lack confidence
or find themselves silenced by a crowd.
Whatever the voice of a particular species
it uses it reliably. I'm sure there is no
elective mute in the world of birds.

Curlew, probing the mud for food,
pausing to make *three slow*
deep whistling notes, accelerating into
a long liquid bubbling or rippling trill,
speak up, explain yourself! But
I'm the inarticulate one, shaking the minidisk,
snapping the pencil lead, thoughts
stubbing against that sound.
Alarm call, breeding, yes yes.
But what are birds saying?

Our best shot is metaphor and mimicry.
Little bit of bread and no cheese.
When our own tongues fail us,
we call on those of our tools and machines.
The Great Tit: *'teacher-teacher'*,
metallic, a saw being sharpened.
Or the Grasshopper Warbler:
a high-pitched, mechanical churring,
the winding of a fishing reel.

Eavesdropping by some frozen field
or sullen river, I imagine birds
are keeping their counsel, guarding the secrets
of their endangered languages,
not to be annexed or colonised . . .

No, that's not it.
Surely they know I'm on their side.
The bird and me: two prisoners
tapping on the pipes.
Longing to connect, but getting only
the syntax, never the meaning,
nothing at all of that.

SOULLESS

Women do not have a soul and do not belong to the human race,
as is shown by many passages of Holy Scripture.
                                    Valens Acidalius, 1595

Anna, when you brought me news
of the bishops' ruling, you trembled.
But I breathed for the first time without fear,
knowing myself to be mortal. I believe the soul
is a kind of swallowed stone. Who would choose
such a bellyful of duty?
Enough that our children survive us;
we need no other tally of our shortcomings.
No wonder our husbands keep grave faces
and refuse to dance. My flesh is my spirit.
I am weightless, running in the barley field,
but he anchors me with a hand on my arm.

Their bodies rot, yet still
the world is littered with their shadows.
More wine, sister! When my time comes,
I'll keep myself company.
I'll leave no ghost, only a smear on the glass.

LOVELL RADIO TELESCOPE,
JODRELL BANK

Clouds scan it at a careful pace,
absorbing its data until they're saturated.
They roll over the fields
and let some of it fall raining onto the grass.
It runs into the earth
with a soft desolate sound.

There's a quiet here, like intelligence.
The cows have a look of wounded surprise
from eating the clever grass,
full of knowledge they don't know how to use.
The buttercups are a special shade of yellow,
unnaturally bright with information.
The trees are more attentive.
Insects make thoughtful moves like chess pieces.

Those clouds are pure whipped memory;
they read and count and store without understanding.
Behind them, a blue which is really darkness
reeling with a million clumsy signals.

THE CURRENCY OF JELLYFISH

for Christina

My parents were paying me sixpence a bucketful
for the bloodless slither and gloop I tipped out
on the grass behind the public convenience.
There had been a mass drowning,
but even death was something they seemed unsure about.
I angled the spade and slid one
like a dead sailor off a plank.
I am the resurrection and the life saith the Lord
and I wouldn't have been surprised if these
already ghosts went slinking back to the sea after dark.

It turned my stomach,
edging the spade in underneath
and handling each corpse to the bucket.
The surprising weight of it, the dead slap it made.
I tested the blade against that unresisting stuff
and shuddered. What must it be like
to have no bones, no guts, just that cloudy blue inside you?
I wobbled on my belly down the beach
with empty jellyfish thoughts, desperate for the sea,
till Mum brought me back with a cheerful wave,
and *Good catch?* said my dad
sprinting by in trunks and goosepimples.

We walked the prom before bed.
Another tide had brought in hundreds more.
They lay like saints,
unharvested, luminous.

NO MAN'S LAND

Poems from the central reservation
of the East Lancashire Road

I

Every day I walk this tightrope of tarmac,
blown toppling in the wake of juggernauts.
I walk it to learn the line of the road,
to keep my place on it.
When I was a lad
my dad took me to a strange part of town,
left me to find the five miles home –
a stiff task that taught me to trust my feet.
In a car, it's all distortion,
one landmark smudging the next:
fast food, do it yourself,
a field with corrugated sheds and a scruffy horse.

I come in, hacking on spent air.
She dishes up meat and gravy
that tastes of diesel. *You're mad*, she says,
the speeds they get up. And in winter.
The soles of my feet are cracked like ancient lino.
The flannel's black when I wash my face at night.
Old fool, she says. *Do you want to end up dead?*
The endless falling cadence of the traffic
swells inside my head and drowns her out.

II

The rag-and-bone man would give away a balloon
in exchange for a broken saucepan
or a coat riddled by moths.
My mum boiled the bones clean for soup first
and kept the best rags for the floor.

There's no currency mean enough round here
for trading in ring-pulls and plastic bottles,
the loops that hold beer cans together,
the polystyrene panels a fridge comes packed in.

You can buy a roll of fifty black sacks for a pound.
They hang flapping in trees and no one bothers to free them.

III

I jump out to try and fix the wiper
then snap it off and feed it to the wind.
The rain deals me such a smack
I think of yachting:
the boom swinging and cracking. Blue.

Back inside, I let the radio drink the battery dry.
Football. Jazz. Gardening quiz.
Lorries josh the car, rock it with mad laughter.
I zip my coat up to the neck,
watch the dark melting down the glass.
There's no one waiting for me at home.

The car snags
then tugs free of its moorings.
Rotating slowly, we're sucked out of bounds.
I smell bladderwrack.

IV

Prayers for guidance across
the scuffed crease of your map;

for a sign
with true diagram and unabridged place names;

for your steady steering,
the bite of tyre on greasy tarmac;

for an open road ahead,
each set of lights nudging the next to green;

for love on full beam
to cut a window in the dark;

and for the suddenness of flowers on the verge:
a riff of colour,
a choice.

V

A butterfly shrugs in Sefton Park

and a tsunami
drowns every lighthouse
from Kirkby to Castlefield.

Again and again
the dark wave arches and shatters.
What help now
on this treacherous spit?

A wrecker's moon rises.